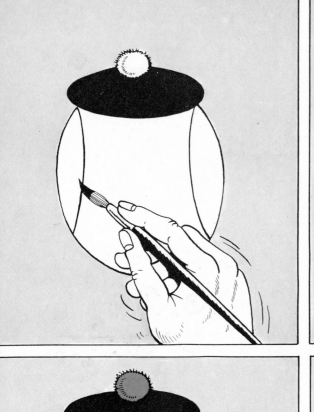

£1.80

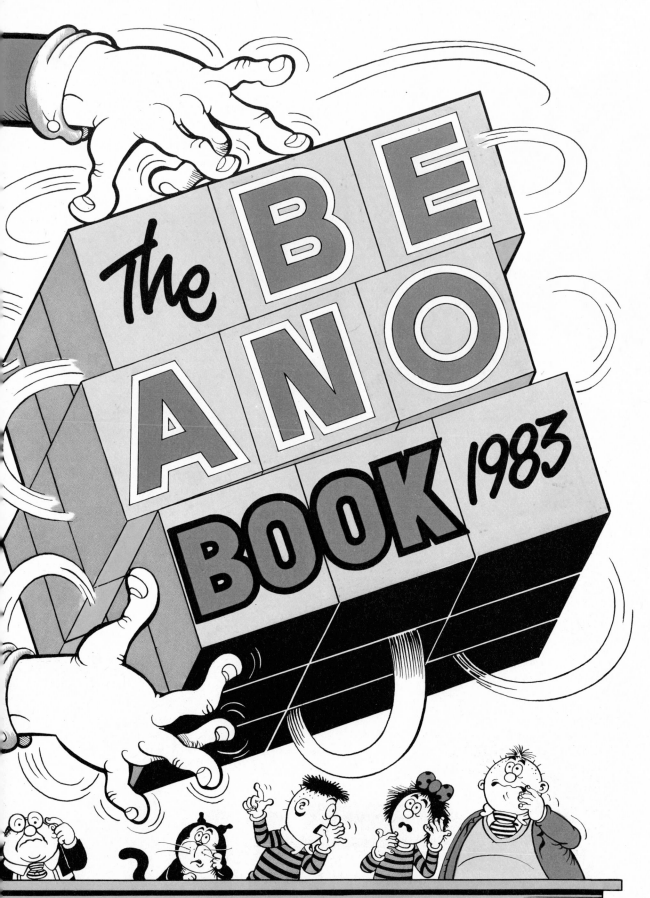

The BEANO BOOK 1983

Printed and Published in Great Britain by D. C. THOMSON & CO., LTD.,
185 Fleet Street, London EC4 2HS. © D. C. THOMSON & CO., LTD., 1982.
ISBN 0 85116 246 0

...and **Minnie THE Minx** is reading it!

GREAT COWBOY AND INDIAN FILM! MUST GO AND FIND MY BOW AND ARROWS!

JUST A MINUTE, MIN!

WAIT AND HEAR THE NEWS. LEARN WHAT'S GOING ON IN THE WORLD.

I HATE THE NEWS—NOTHING INTERESTING EVER HAPPENS!

NEWS

TODAY ARNOLD BLODGETT HIT HIS THUMB WITH A HAMMER!

After the news—

BORING OLD NEWS!

WONDER WHAT'S ON THAT BIT OF PAPER?

SO FATTY'S ON A DIET—THAT IS NEWS!

FATTY'S DIET
NO SWEETS
NO CAKE
NO PORRIDGE
NO CUSTARD
NO POP
NO MINCE
NO SOUP
NO DIET FOR ME!

HMMM! I COULD DO WITH A NEW NEST.

NOT MUCH THAT'S NEWSWORTHY HERE.

Below you'll see a sleepy P.C.!

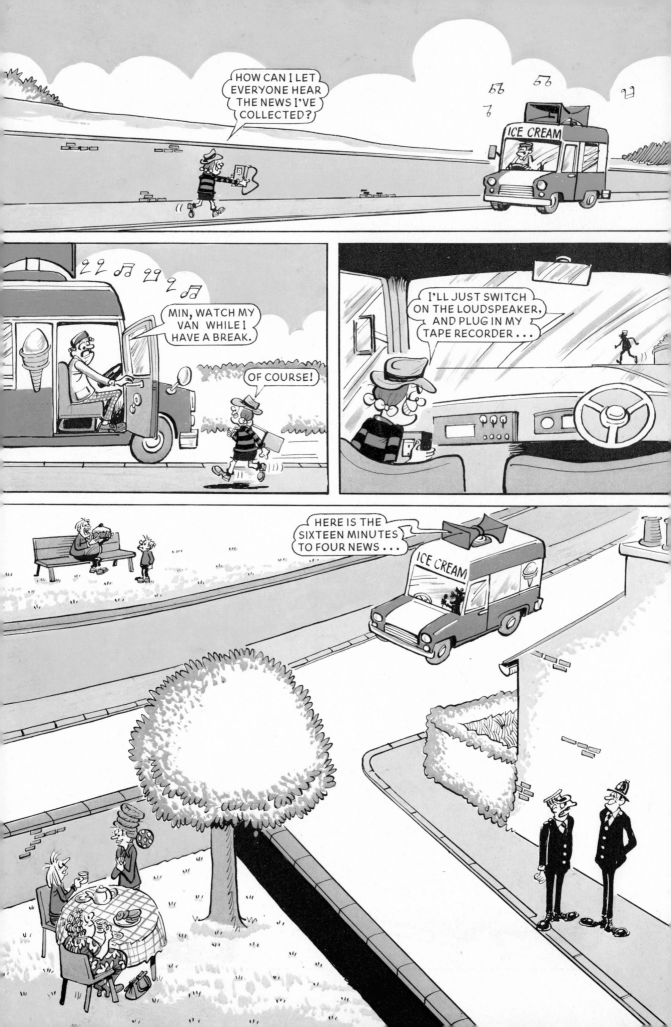

Tell-tale loud hail!

A white fright!

BILLY WHIZZ

Poor Billy's never felt so silly!

DENNIS *the* MENACE and GNASHER

WHO'S A CLEVER FOO-FOO? WHO CAN DO LOTS OF TRICKS THEN?

YAH! LET'S SEE!

SEE? FOO-FOO IS BEGGING!

THAT'S NOTHING-GNASHER CAN BEG, TOO. SHOW HIM, GNASHER!

NOD NOD

Take note of Gnasher's coat!

Well I never—very clever!

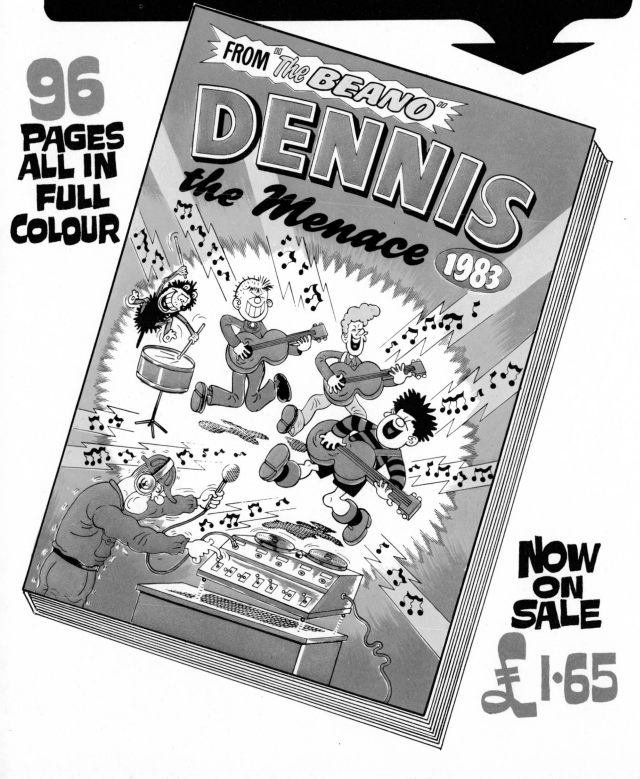

A perfect throw with a ball of snow!

LITTLE PLUM

COOKIE'S GONE ON HOLIDAY— I NEED UM VOLUNTEER TO DO UM COOKING.

WONDER WHO IT WILL BE?

ME? OH, NO!

WHAT DO I KNOW ABOUT COOKING?

Mad Dad!

White fright!

Beware, beware of that dazzling glare!

Drop stop!

I'VE LOST MY SHEEP!

HERE IT IS!

WAH!

Soon—

ER—THERE HAS BEEN A SLIGHT CHANGE TO OUR PROGRAMME . . .

SMUDGE'S MUM

I'M LOOKING FORWARD TO SEEING SMUDGE AS A WHITE FLUFFY SHEEP.

BAA, BAA, BLACK SHEEP, HAVE YOU ANY WOOL? . . .

. . . YES, SIR! YES, SIR! THREE BAGS FULL!

SMUDGE ALWAYS WAS THE BLACK SHEEP OF THE FAMILY!

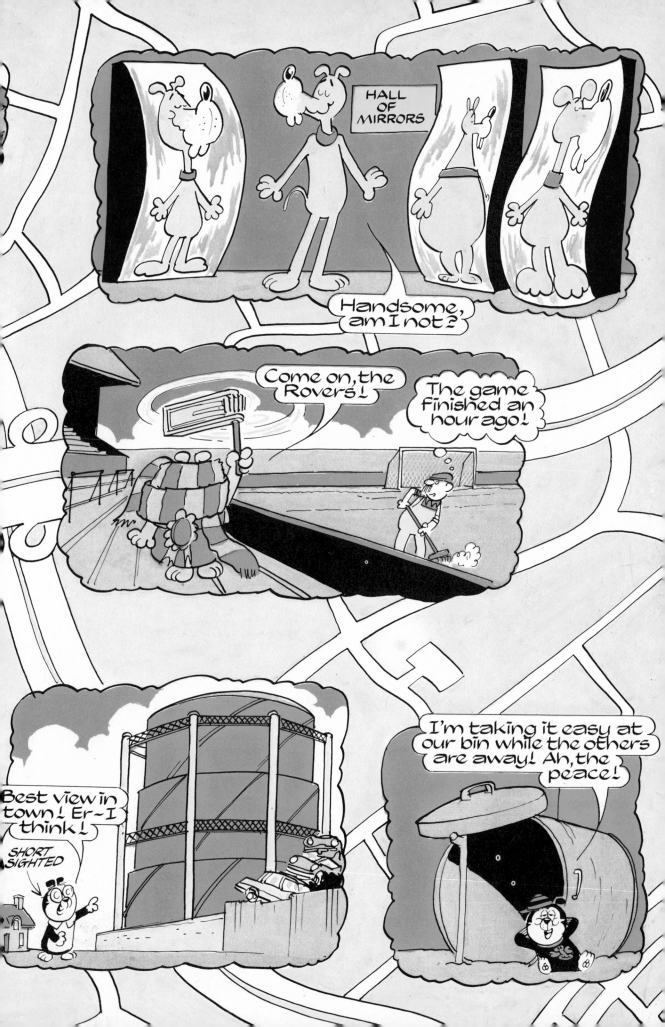

More fun with Bandit Number One!

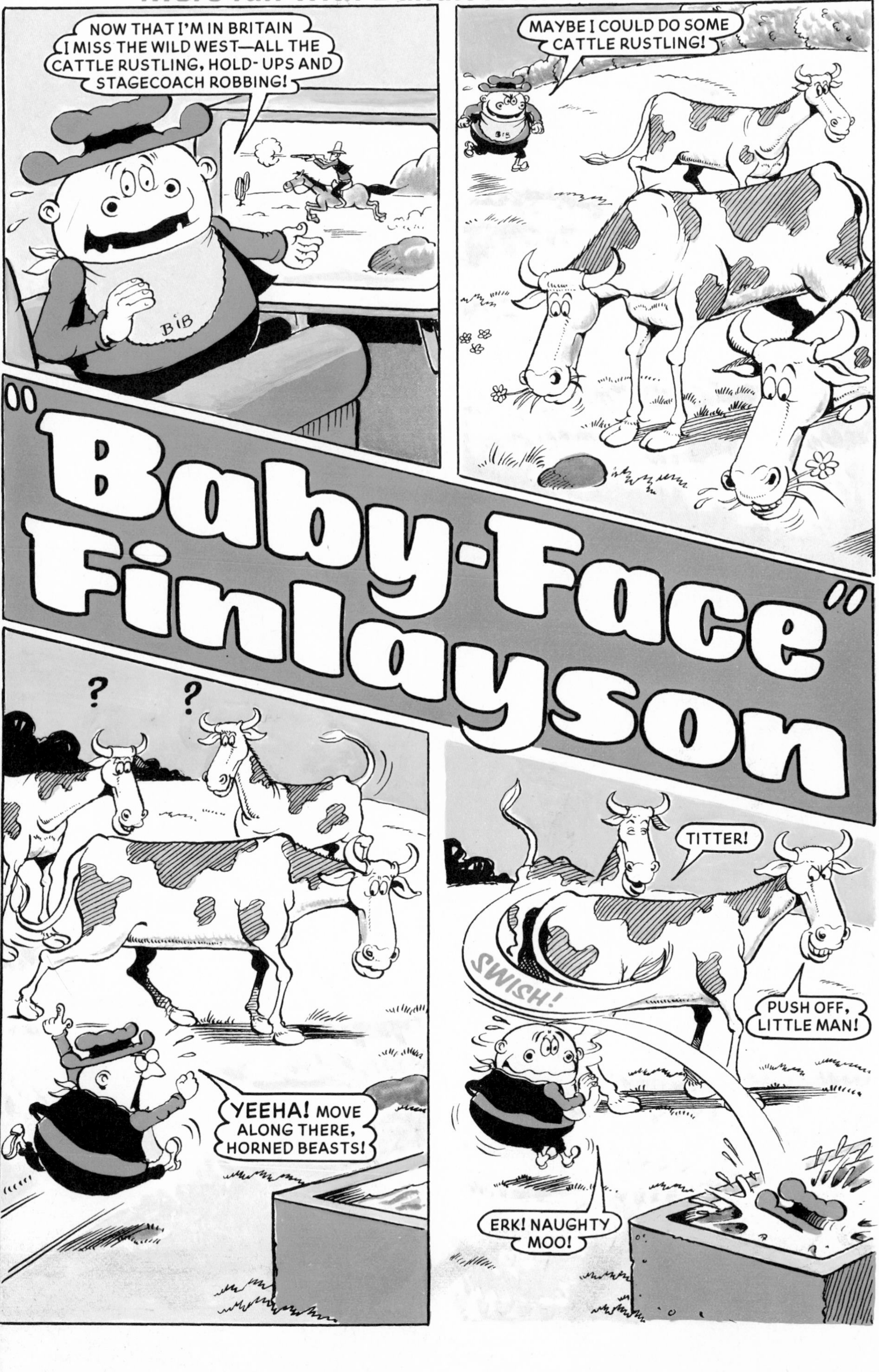

PICTURE SHOW

"BOWL OF FRUIT"
BY FATTY (BASH ST.)

"SELF-PORTRAIT"
BY PLUG (BASH ST.)

"LANDSCAPE"
BY 'ERBERT (BASH ST.)
(SO SHORT-SIGHTED
HE MISSED THE CANVAS)

"MY GRAN"
BY WILFRID (BASH ST.)

"SUNSET" BY GRANDPA
(TOOK SO LONG HE MISSED IT)

"SON RISE"
BY DENNIS'S DAD

"INDIAN SUMMER"
BY LITTLE PLUM

"WATERFALL"
BY SMIFFY (BASH ST.)

"THE LAUGHING CAVALIER"
BY MINNIE THE MINX
(HE DIDN'T LIKE HER JOKES)

Tom Dick and Sally

More charging and barging!

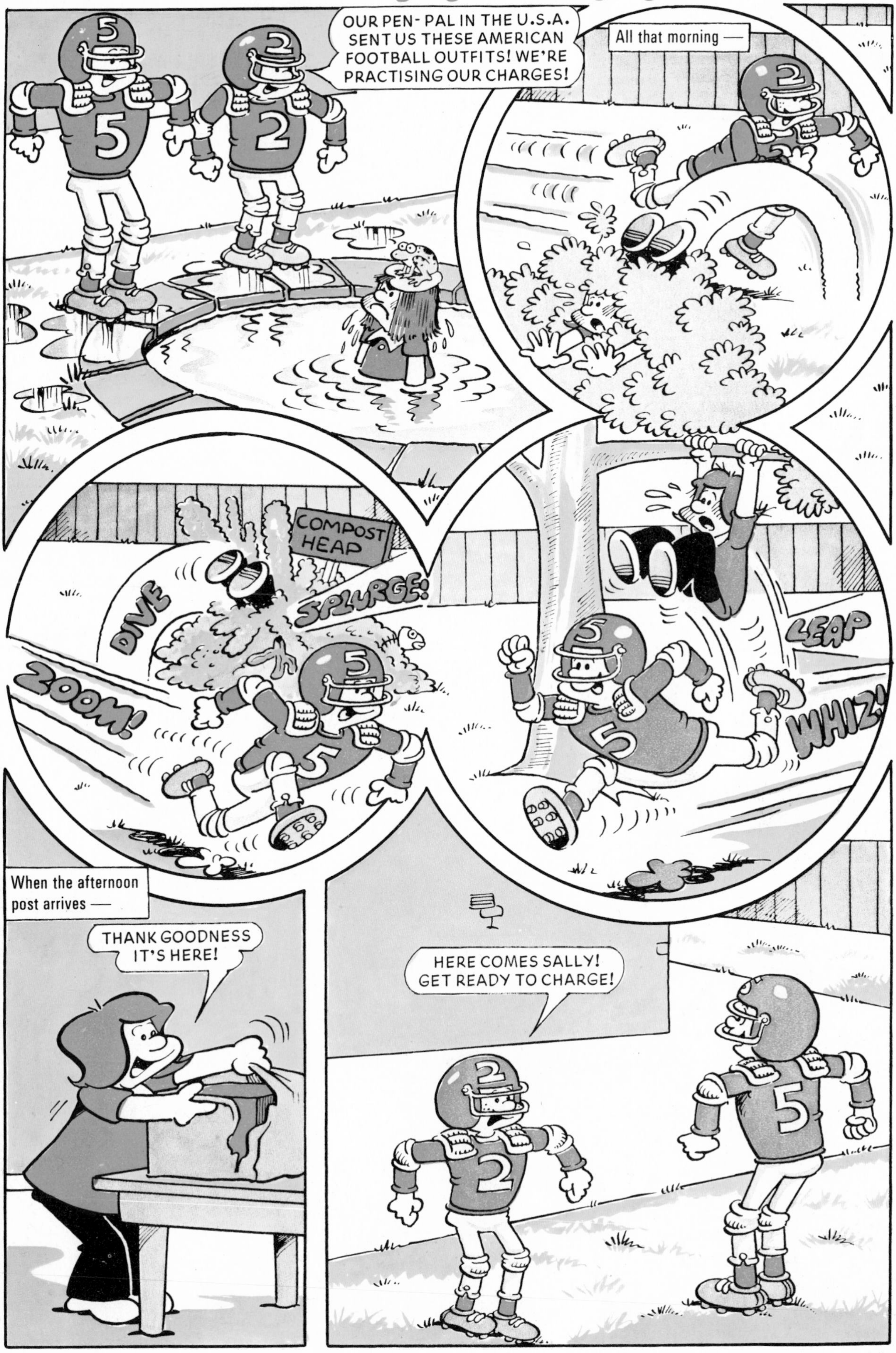

The BASH STREET KIDS in SLIDE SHOW

I'LL GIVE YOU A LITTLE TREAT TODAY...

BORED

BONK!

...I'LL SHOW YOU MY HOLIDAY SNAPS FROM LAST YEAR!

GROAN!

NOT AGAIN!

THUMP!

BAH!

I'LL PUT THE FIRST ONE IN UPSIDE DOWN— THAT SHOULD MAKE THEM TAKE NOTICE!

OH, DEAR! SILLY ME! I'VE PUT IT IN UPSIDE DOWN. HA-HA!

DEAD SILENCE!

HMM! NOT A LOT OF REACTION TO THAT, WAS THERE?

YOU ALWAYS PUT THE FIRST SLIDE IN UPSIDE DOWN, TEACHER!

WE'VE COME TO EXPECT IT!

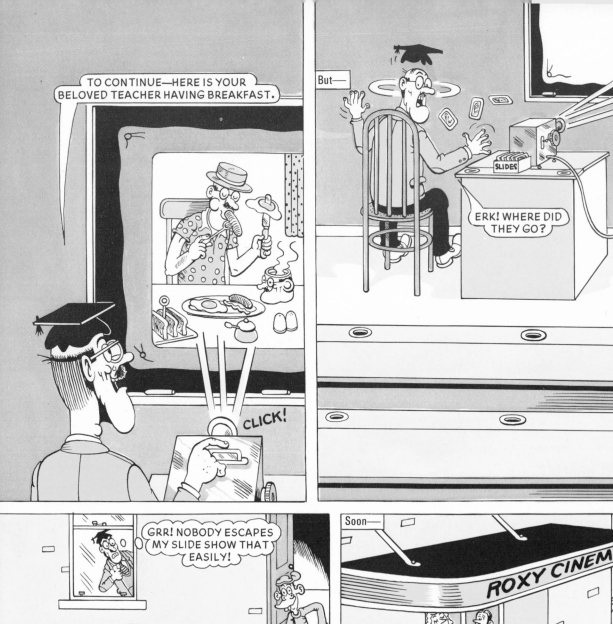

Look what's seen on the screen!

Inside—

I WONDER WHAT THE MAIN FEATURE IS TODAY?

Then—

OH, NO! THE CINEMA'S SHOWING TEACHER'S SLIDES!

In the projection room—

I SAID I'D TAKE OVER TO LET THE PROJECTIONIST HAVE A REST. HAR-HAR!

CLICK!

SLIDES

ROXY CINEMA

SNOOZE!

SNOW GREY LAUNDRY

ROXY CINE

NEXT WEEK

LET'S HIDE IN THE LAUNDRY! TEACHER WON'T FIND US HERE!

OH, YES I WILL!

Projector protector!

School Sports

CHOMP! CHOMP!

Fatty won the tug-of-war—
The cup he proudly lifted.
The seven dumplings in his tum
Made sure he wasn't shifted!

Spotty won the shot-putt crown—
Not bad for one so small.
The crafty fellow swapped his shot
For a big black rubber ball!

Wilfrid laughed and danced around—
At what had he come best?
In fact, the reason for his mirth
Was his new hairy vest!

FLIP! FLAP! FLIP! FLAP!

Plug he was the one mile champ—
You should have seen him go!
He said that if he flapped his ears
He ran just like Seb Coe!

To win the flat race Danny tied
A toy plane on each shoe.
But they were faster then he thought—
My gosh, he fairly flew!

The sack race it was won by Toots—
She whistled down the track.
She owed her runaway success
To hornets in her sack!

Smiffy was a worried lad —
Asked Toots "What's up with you?"
He said," Next's the three-legged race,
And I have only two!"

'Erbert was the pole-vault king—
You've never seen the likes.
He didn't have to use a pole—
He sat on Danny's spikes!

Slow cycling was won by Sid.
He said," It was just luck!
I cycled through a patch of mud
And both my wheels got stuck!"

DORIS, THE SCHOOL ← CLEANER

THE BASH STREET KIDS in "CLEAN THAT CLASSROOM!"

TRING! TRING!

PLAYTIME!

BACK, YOU TERRORS!

ERK!

Yes! Yes! Yes!—a frightful mess!

Poor machine—feeling green!

Shock in store—on the floor!

The fun's around with Dennis's hound!

GNASHER'S TALE

TIME FOR A SNOOZE . . . I'LL SHARE MY KENNEL WITH YOU.

GNEE! GNEE! I'LL SLEEP INSIDE . . .

. . . YOU SLEEP OUTSIDE! HUH!

Later—

AHA! A CAT! I'LL SHARE IT WITH YOU!

YOU CAN HAVE FIRST CHASE!

YAP! YAP!

MEEOW!

READER'S VOICE

SO KIND OF YOU, GNASHER!

LORD SNOOTY

A TV FILM CREW IS COMING TO DO A PROGRAMME ON BUNKERTON CASTLE TODAY!

Later—

AH, THEY'VE ARRIVED!

WE'LL START FILMING IN THE GREAT HALL . . .

ER—I WOULDN'T GO OVER THERE . . .

. . . THE FLOOR'S ROTTEN!

AARGH!

CRUNCH!

CRACK!

Then—

WE'LL HAVE YOU OFF TO HOSPITAL SOON! AND YOU'LL BE PLEASED TO KNOW THE CAMERA'S UNDAMAGED!

BIG DEAL!

CHRISTMAS GREETINGS WITH A LAUGH FOR THE "BEANO" OFFICE STAFF!

FROM MINNIE

BERET CHRISTMAS

CHRISTMAS ~~REPORT~~ CARD

FROM ROGER

FROM BILLY WHIZZ (HE ALWAYS LIKES TO BE AHEAD OF EVERYBODY ELSE!)

CHRISTMAS WISHES *for* NEXT YEAR

FROM PLUG → (THE POSTIE REFUSED TO DELIVER THIS!)

MERRY CHRISTMAS
THIS IS A PIECE OF THE POSTMAN'S TROUSERS— Dennis

Merry Christmas

FROM GNASHER

It's time those sheep went to sleep!

GRANDPA

I'M GOING TO FEEL EMBARRASSED ABOUT THIS—I KNOW I AM!

COME ON—HEEL, BOY!

Soon—

OH, DEAR!

NNN!

NO! STOP! YOU MUSTN'T CHASE THAT CAT!

TUG!

EH?

Then—

GULP! THIS COULD MEAN TROUBLE!

DENNIS the MENACE and PIE-FACE

A TYPICAL DAY IN THE LIFE OF MY PAL, PIE-FACE, STARTS WHEN HE STUMBLES DOWNSTAIRS FOR BREAKFAST...

...WHICH CONSISTS OF PORRIDGE PIES!

MUNCH! SLURP!

SQUELCH!

My, oh my—a golden pie!

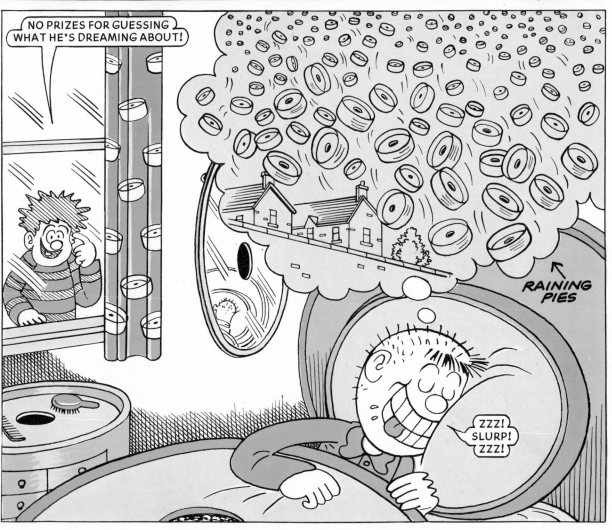

SPOT-THE-

CAN YOU SPOT THE TEN DELIBERATE MISTAKES THE "BEANO" ARTIST HAS MADE IN DRAWING THESE "BEANO" CHARACTERS? ANSWERS AT FOOT OF NEXT PAGE.

WORLD CUP

Roger the Dodger

JUST A MINUTE, ROGER!

BET MUM'S GOT A NASTY JOB FOR ME!

TAKE MY ENTRY TO THE FLOWER SHOW, SON.

ULP! NASTIER THAN I FEARED!

CAN'T WALK PAST MY PALS WITH THESE! I NEED A QUICK DODGE!

TALKING ABOUT THE "DENNIS THE MENACE" BOOK 1983 (NOW ON SALE)

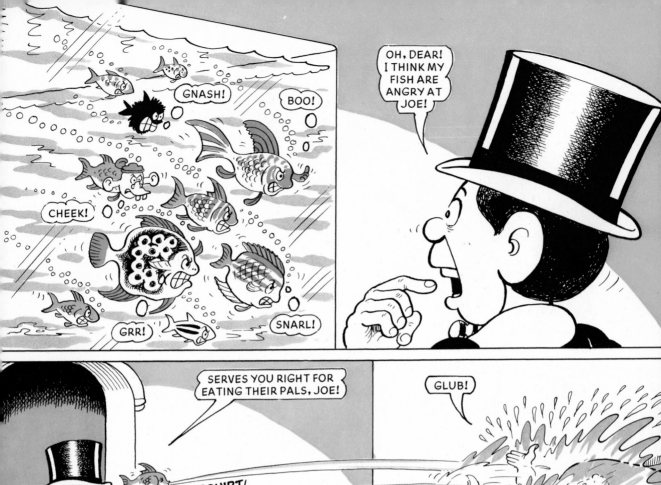

Below you'll see a tired B.B.!

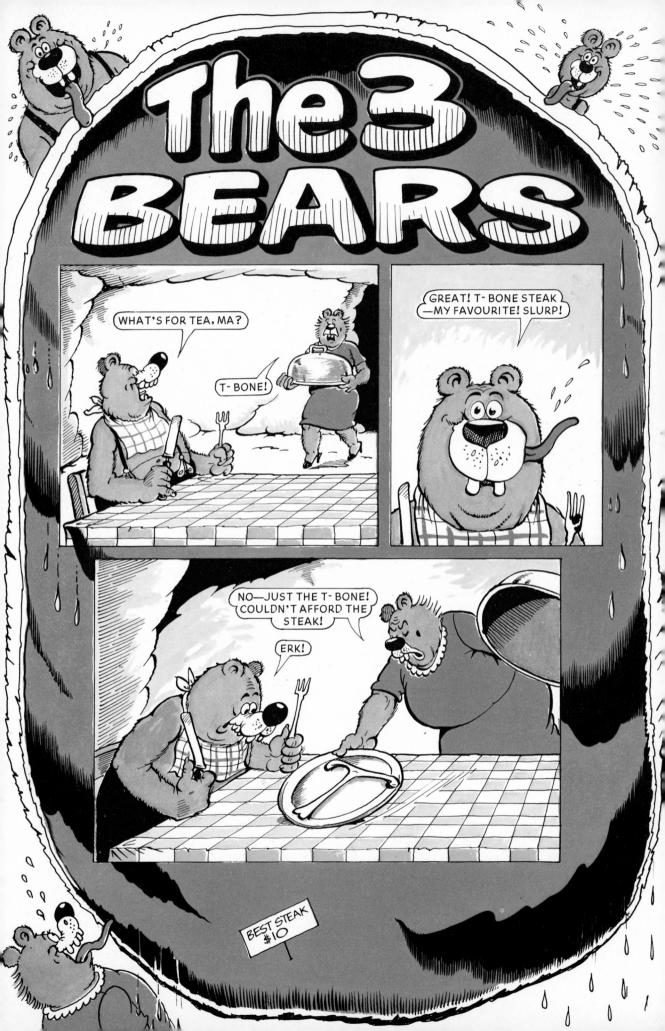

A strange feed for bears in need!

LITTLE PLUM

IT'S CHRISTMAS EVE!

Just then—

WALLY WALLY WOOSKA!

EEK! OUR ENEMIES, UM PUTTYFEET TRIBE, ARE ON UM WARPATH!

HOI! STOP!

YOU MUST BE JOKING!

LEAP!

HOP!

COME BACK, PLUM!

SLIDE

I'LL SLIDE DOWNHILL TO SAFETY!

WHEEE!

THEY WON'T CATCH ME NOW!

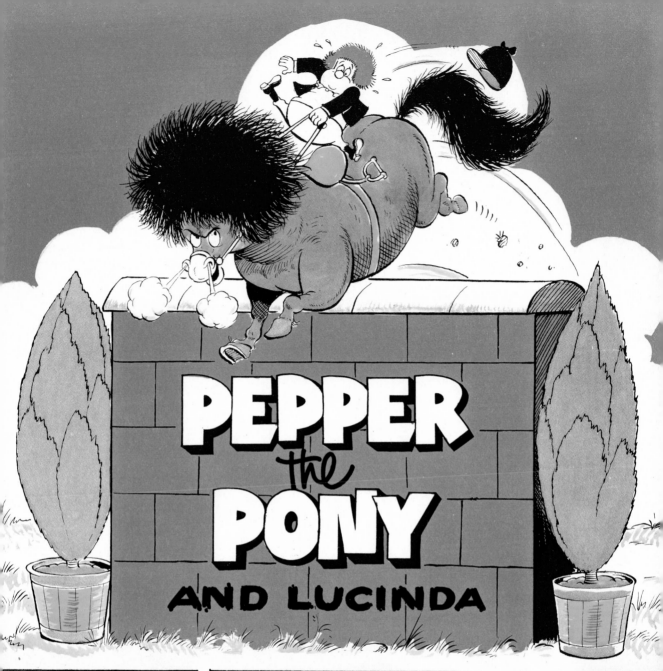

PEPPER the PONY
AND LUCINDA

MY PONY, PEPPER, WILL DO ANYTHING FOR A SUGAR LUMP.

SUGAR LUMPS

SEE WHAT I MEAN?

CARTWHEEL

CARTWHEEL

SUGAR LUMPS

Lumps make bumps!

Minnie the Minx

HEY! CAN I PLAY FOOTBALL WITH YOU? I FEEL LIKE A GAME!

Tripping and ripping!

I'M PRETTY GOOD AT AVOIDING A TACKLE!

TELL YOU WHAT— I COULD PLAY IN GOAL!

I'M GREAT AT DIVING...

...AND PUNCHING OUT THE BALL...OOPS! SORRY!

BOP!

What a shame—end of game!

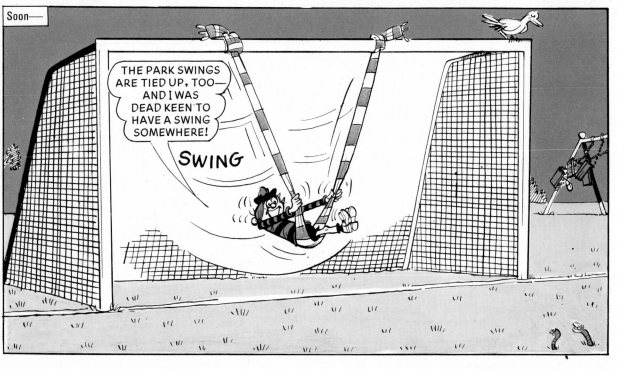

GNASHER'S TALE

I REMEMBER BEING EXTRA-HOT AFTER CHASING CATS...

IT'S LUCKY DAD MADE A DOGGIE TAP FOR ME!

TURN

SWOOSH!

Then—

♪

BUTCHER

AHA!

EEK!

ZOOM!

GNASH! GNASH!

Much chasing later—

GNEE! GNEE!

FINISHED THIS "BEANO BOOK", HAVE YOU? BUT THE FUN'S NOT OVER YET—YOU CAN
CARRY ON LAUGHING
AT YOUR FAVOURITE FUNNY FOLK RIGHT HERE!
THE BEANO
OUT EVERY WEEK OF THE YEAR
DENNIS THE MENACE
SWEET SHOP
SOFTIES
WONDER IF THAT WOULD WORK WITH US? WE'LL GIVE IT A TRY— WE'LL BE GOOD FOR A CHANGE!

OVERSEAS READERS!
We can send " The BEANO "
to you every week!

Send for details to:—

Subscribers' Dept.,
D.C. Thomson & Co., Ltd.,
12 Bank Street,
DUNDEE, U.K.
DD1 9HU.